badminton

consultant

DR. JAMES L. BREEN
Chairman, Department of
 Physical Education
George Washington University
Washington, D.C.

demonstrator

LARRY SABEN
1967 National Junior Singles,
 Boy's Doubles, and
 Mixed Doubles Champion
1969 National Senior Mixed
 Double Champion Member,
 Thomas Cup Team

ST. PHILIPS COLLEGE LIBRARY

published by:
The Athletic Institute
Merchandise Mart, Chicago

*A not-for-profit organization
devoted to the advancement of
athletics, physical education
and recreation.*

© *The Athletic Institute 1969*
All Rights Reserved

796.345
B136
1969

**Library of Congress
Catalog Card Number 79-109498**

**"Sports Techniques" Series
SBN·87670-035-0**

*Published by The Athletic Institute
Chicago, Illinois 60654*

foreword

"Sports Techniques" is but one item in a comprehensive list of sports instructional aids made available on a non-profit basis by The Athletic Institute. The photographic material in this book has been reproduced in total from The Athletic Institute's loop film series. This book is a part of a program designed to bring the many benefits of athletics, physical education and recreation to everyone.

The Athletic Institute is a non-profit organization devoted to the advancement of athletics, physical education and recreation. The Institute believes that participation in athletics and recreation has benefits of inestimable value to the individual and to the community.

The nature and scope of the many Institute programs are determined by an advisory committee, whose members are noted for their outstanding knowledge, experience and ability in the fields of athletics, physical education and recreation.

The Institute believes that through this book the reader will become a better badminton player, skilled in the fundamentals of this fine game. Knowledge, and the practice necessary to mold knowledge into playing ability, are the keys to real enjoyment of playing badminton.

The lifetime game of badminton aids in development of motor skill, flexibility, agility and endurance as well as providing enjoyable recreation.

The Athletic Institute

TABLE OF CONTENTS

PAGE

GRIP AND COCKING 5
   Gripping 6
   And Cocking 7

FOOTWORK 8
   Starting Position 8
   1 O'Clock – 3 O'Clock Positions 8
   9 O'Clock – 11 O'Clock Positions 9
   5 O'Clock – 7 O'Clock Positions 9

SERVES 10
   High Deep Serves 10
   Low Short Serve 11
   Drive Serve 12
   Flick Serve 13

OVERHEAD SHOTS 14
   Forehand Overhead Shots 15
   Defensive Clear 15
   Attacking Clear 16
   Smash 16
   Drop 17
   Backhand Overhead Shots 17
   Defensive Clears 18
   Attacking Clears 18
   Smash 19
   Drop 19
   Drive Shots 20

UNDERHAND CLEAR SHOTS 21
   Underhand Clear Shots 21
   Backhand Clear Shot 22

NET SHOTS 22
   Backhand 23

AROUND-THE-HEAD-SHOTS 24

RULES SIMPLIFIED 25
   The Laws of Badminton 27
   Some Common Badminton Terms 41
   Playing Better Badminton 46
   Notes 47

BADMINTON COURT

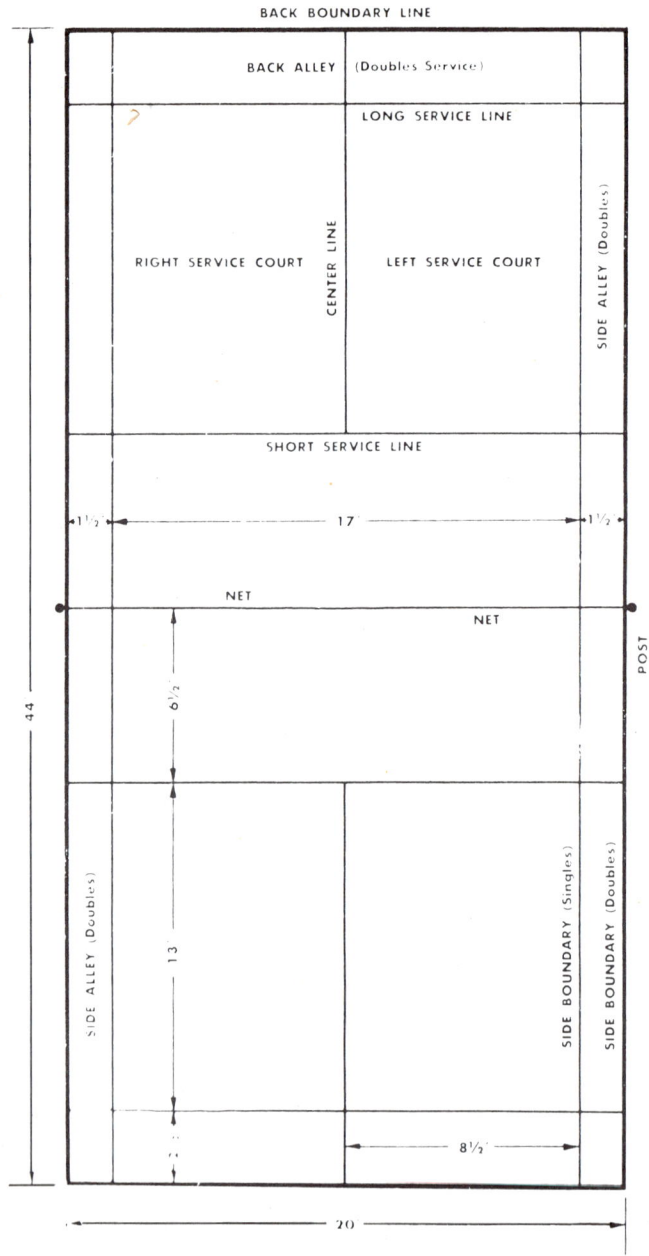

grip and cocking

The Grip is a combination of gripping and holding. The handle of the racket is placed diagonally across the last three fingers which grip, and encircled by the thumb and index finger which hold. The racket is COCKED for the forehand stroke by rotating the forearm clockwise. The forearm is rotated counter-clockwise for a backhand cocking position.

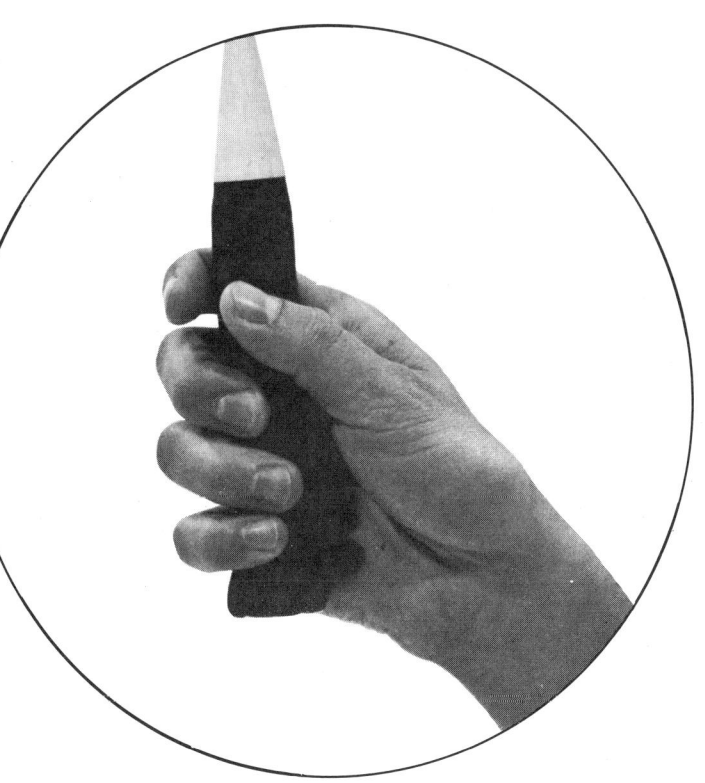

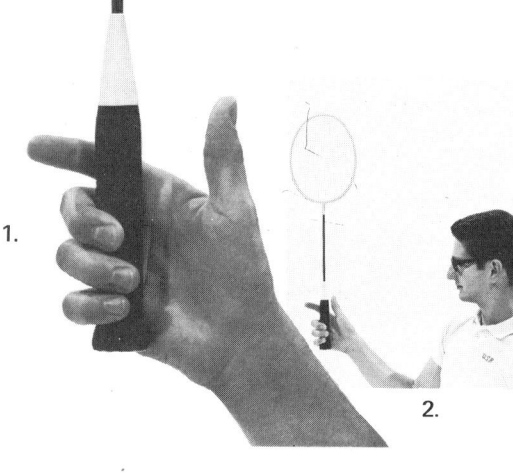

GRIPPING

1. Place palm parallel to racket face.

2. GRIPPING FINGERS — racket handle diagonally across the last three fingers.

3. HOLDING FINGERS — encircle handle with thumb and index finger to combine GRIPPING and HOLDING.

4. "V" slightly to LEFT OF CENTER — for forehand grip the "V," formed by thumb and index finger, is slightly to the left on the top of the racket handle.

5. BACKHAND GRIP — fingers grip as in forehand but thumb is moved behind racket.

COCKING — rotate forearm clockwise for forehand stroke.

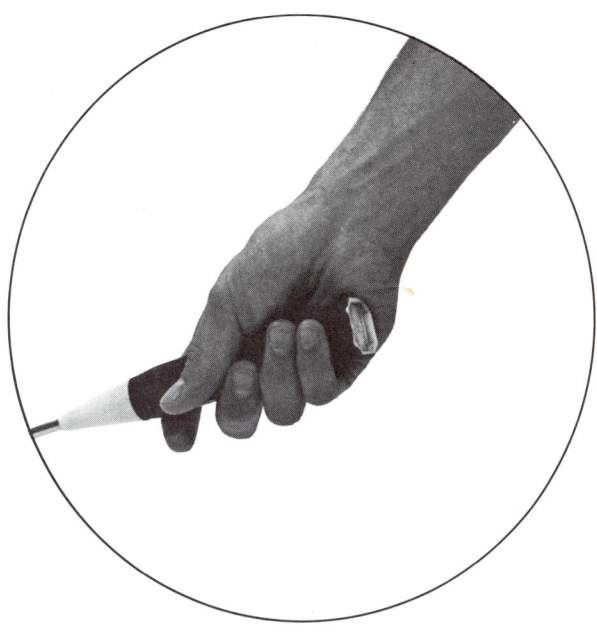

and COCKING

1.

2.

3.

1. BACKHAND COCKING — rotate forearm counter-clockwise.

2. OVERHEAD COCKING

3. FOREHAND COCKING

4. UNDERHAND COCKING — (Proper cocking action for these strokes)

4.

5.

footwork

STARTING POSITION

The player must start from a constantly maintained READY position in order to move properly on the court. The correct stance is similar to that of a baseball infielder expecting a grounder. The weight should be on the balls of the feet. The feet are apart about shoulder width to assure good balance. The body is relaxed with the knees slightly flexed. Both arms are held in front of the body. The racket head should be about shoulder height.

1 O'CLOCK – 3 O'CLOCK POSITIONS

Movement to the right, for a forehand stroke at these positions on the court, involves moving the center of gravity in the direction of the shuttle. Step to the right, slide the other foot in the same direction, simultaneously rotate the body to prepare for stroking.

9 O'CLOCK — 11 O'CLOCK POSITIONS

Movement to the left, for the backhand stroke at these positions on the court, involves moving the center of gravity in the direction of the shuttle. Move the left foot toward the shuttle. Cross over the right foot. Rotate the body and prepare to stroke with the back to the net.

5 O'CLOCK — 7 O'CLOCK POSITIONS

To reach these back court positions a player may use either of the footwork techniques:

1) FACING NET, BACK PEDAL
2) TURN, SHIFT CENTER OF GRAVITY, SLIDE

serves

HIGH DEEP SERVES

This serve is an underhand forehand serve hit high so that the shuttle will land in deep court, near the back line.

HIGH DEEP SERVES (Continued)

1.
2.
3.
4.

STARTING POSITION — Both feet in contact with floor. Body stationary. Shuttle held in front of body.

HIGH DEEP SERVE — Rotate body. Shift weight to front foot. Contact shuttle in front of body.

SHUTTLE CONTACT FOR LEGAL SERVE — top of racket must be below server's hand.

UNCOCK WRIST — upon contacting shuttle.

FOLLOW THROUGH — racket follows through to insure full power for stroke.

LOW SHORT SERVE

This serve should be made so that the shuttle has a flat trajectory. The shuttle just clears the net and falls close to the short service line.

The techniques for the LOW SHORT SERVE are the same as those for the HIGH DEEP SERVE.

LOW DEEP SERVES (Continued)

STARTING POSITION — Both feet in contact with floor. Body stationary. Shuttle held in front of body. Shift weight to front foot.

STROKING — This is a PUSH type serve — wrist remains almost fully cocked with little rotation of forearm. Contact shuttle near waist height. Obtain flat trajectory.

DRIVE SERVE

The DRIVE SERVE is comparable to hitting a line drive in baseball. This serve should be driven just below the opponent's shoulders.

All basic techniques for the DRIVE SERVE are the same as the HIGH DEEP SERVE.

1. 2. 3.

1. STARTING POSITION

2. ROTATE BODY

3. SHIFT WEIGHT

EXCEPT — the hand is partially uncocked at contact with the shuttle.

Since the hand does not go beyond half cock, the follow-through is a limited arc.

FLICK SERVE

This serve is one of the better deception shots used mainly in doubles and mixed doubles play. It is used when the opponent rushes the net on LOW SHORT SERVES.

FLICK SERVES (Continued)

The same basic techniques apply as to STARTING POSITION, ARM POSITION, BODY ROTATION, WEIGHT SHIFT —

EXCEPT — the serve appears to be a LOW SHORT SERVE, since the forearm is cocked fully when approaching the shuttle. At the instant before contact, the forearm is rotated to flick the shuttle over the opponent's head. The follow-through is restricted.

overhead shots

FOREHAND AND BACKHAND, ATTACKING and DEFENSIVE CLEARS, SMASH and DROP

FOREHAND OVERHEAD SHOTS

Forehand overhead shots begin with the weight on the back foot followed by shifting the weight to the front foot. The body rotates during the action.

DEFENSIVE CLEAR

To insure a high trajectory, angle the racket backward. Contact shuttle high and in front of body. The high, deep shot allows enough time to assume proper court position as a receiver.

ATTACKING CLEAR

Basically, the same shot as a DEFENSIVE CLEAR

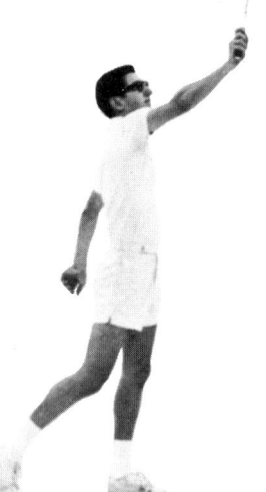

EXCEPT — the racket head is perpendicular to t[he] floor at contact, which flattens the trajectory. This [is] a quick hit used primarily to place the shuttle de[ep] and out of reach of the opponent.

SMASH

1.　　　　　　**2.**

Lead with the elbow. Rotate body. Arm straight at contact. Follow through.

Body faces net at completion of shot.

This shot is an extension of t[he] overhead clear — and SHOUL[D] LOOK LIKE the CLEAR — un[til] contact is made with the shuttl[e.] Contact is made further in front [of] the body. The racket is angle[d] slightly forward.

DROP

FAST DROP — racket at basically same angle as smash. Shot is hit like smash.

EXCEPT — with softer touch at contact with shuttle.

LOOP DROP — racket angle is similar to defensive clear. Shuttle should drop in looping fashion near net on opponent's side.

Effective drop shots land close to the net.

BACKHAND OVERHEAD SHOTS

Backhand overhead shots are executed with the player's back to the net. The forearm is bent toward the chest for the "ready" position.

Extend the arm. Rotate the forearm clockwise simultaneously at contact with the shuttle.

DEFENSIVE CLEARS

Angle racket slightly backward for a high trajectory. Contact shuttle high and just in front of body. High, deep flight of shuttle permits time for player to assume proper court position as receiver.

ATTACKING CLEARS

Basically same shot as Defensive Cle

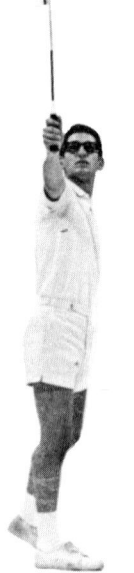

EXCEPT — racket head is perpendicular to floor contact. The trajectory is flattened.

This is a quick hit used primarily to place the bi deep and out of reach of the opponent.

SMASH

This shot is an extension of the OVERHEAD CLEAR — and SHOULD LOOK LIKE the CLEAR — until contact is made with the shuttle.

Lead with elbow. Rotate body. Arm straight on contact. Contact the shuttle further in front of body than in OVERHEAD CLEAR. Angle racket slightly forward.

DROP

FAST DROP — racket at basically the same angle as SMASH at contact. Shot is hit like SMASH

EXCEPT — with softer touch at contact with shuttle.

LOOP DROP — racket angle similar to that of a Defensive Clear. Shuttle should drop in looping fashion near net on opponent's side.

Lead with elbow. Straighten arm at contact. Back toward net.

DRIVE SHOTS

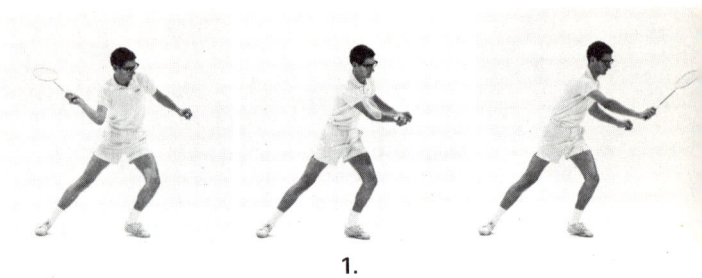

1.

The shuttle is hit quickly, forehand or backhand with a flat trajectory. Shot is hit deep to permit regaining normal receiving position.

1.

FOREHAND DRIVE — Similar to throwing a baseball sidearm. Lead with elbow. Hit from cocked position. Arm straight at contact with shuttle.

2.

BACKHAND DRIVE — Lead with elbow. Arm straight at contact with shuttle. Rotate forearm and follow through.

underhand clear shots

UNDERHAND CLEAR SHOTS

FOREHAND UNDERHAND CLEAR — Weight transfers to front foot. Shuttle stroked in front of body. Uncock arm at contact to hit shuttle in high, deep trajectory. Swing up and through. Follow through.

BACKHAND CLEAR SHOT

BACKHAND CLEAR SHOT — Weight on front foot. Elbow leads. Contact shuttle in front of body. Uncock at contact to hit shuttle in high, deep trajectory. Swing up and through. Follow through.

net shots

Net shots require a delicate touch. The racket is held more loosely. Shot is sometimes called a "hairpin" drop.

NET SHOTS (Continued)

FOREHAND — Contact shuttle near top of net. Stretch and reach for shuttle.

BACKHAND

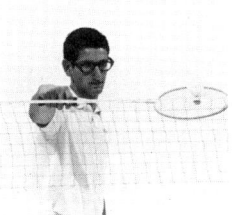

BACKHAND — When hitting use whole arm motion rather than forearm rotation. Stretch and reach for shuttle.

around-the-head-shots

Such shots are within an arc around the head, above the shoulder and on the left side of body.

Body faces net. Weight on front foot at contact. Rotate arm. Angle racket face to produce CLEAR, DROP, or SMASH. Follow through by stepping forward.

RULES SIMPLIFIED

he laws of the International Badminton
ederation, adapted by the American Bad-
inton Association, are the official rules of
he game. Some of them, however, may be a
ttle complicated so here are Pam, Sue, Bob
nd Barry to explain the **basic** playing rules.

Every badminton game starts with a service. The person serving is called the "in" side. Here Pam is the server or "in" side. The receiver must stand with both feet within her service court and in contact with the floor until her racket hits the bird. Any violation of a rule is called a "fault". The server and the player served to must stand within the limits of their respective service-courts (as bounded by the short and long service, the center, and side lines), and some part of both feet of these players must remain in contact with the ground in a stationary position until the service is delivered. A foot on or touching a line in the case of either the server or the receiver shall be held to be outside his service court The respective partners may take up any position, provided they do not unsight or otherwise obstruct an opponent.

It's a fault if she steps over or touches any boundary line of the service court until after the bird has been hit.

It's a fault while serving if the head of her racket is above her waist when she hits the bird.

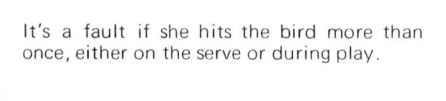

It's a fault if she hits the bird more than once, either on the serve or during play.

THE LAWS OF BADMINTON

ts

a fault:

f in serving, the shuttle at the instant of
g struck be higher than the server's
t, or if any part of the head of the
et, at the instant of striking the shuttle,
igher than any part of the server's hand
ing the racket.

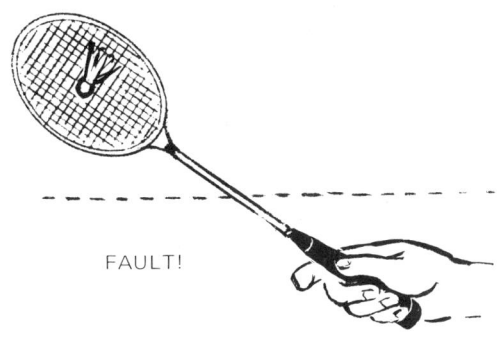

FAULT!

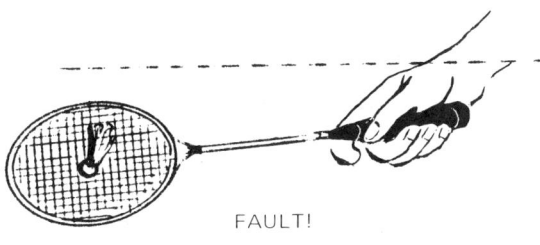

FAULT!

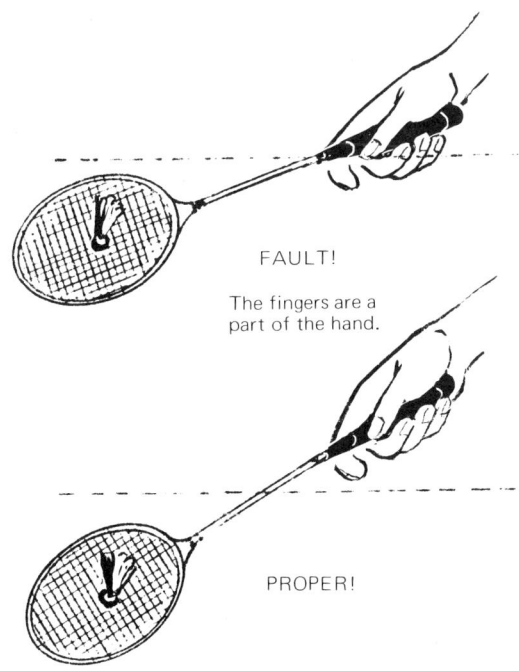

FAULT!

The fingers are a part of the hand.

PROPER!

It is not a fault, and is not counted as a try, if she swings at the bird and misses completely in her service.

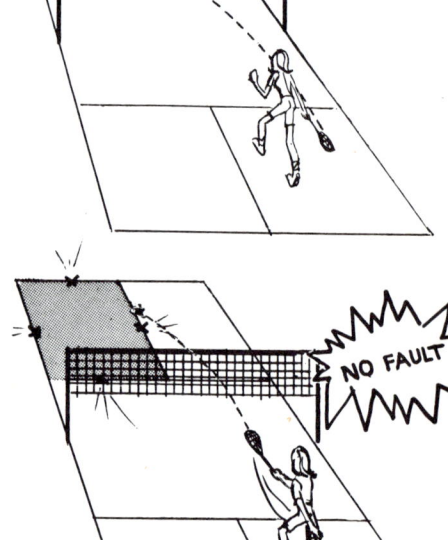

On her service, Pam must hit the bird into the service court diagonally opposite. If the bird falls anywhere outside this court, it is a fault against Pam.

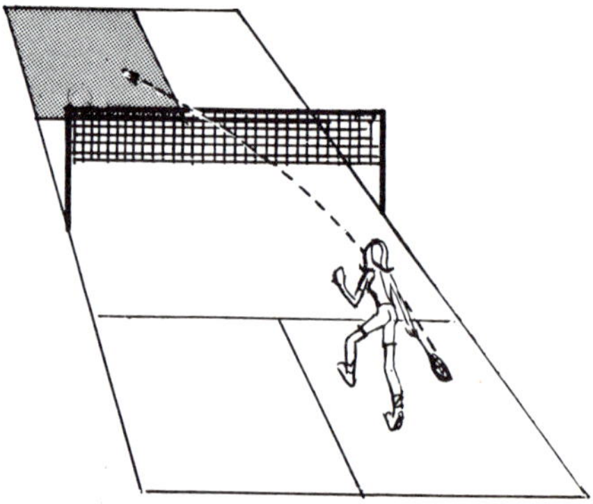

But it is not a fault if it falls on any of the boundary lines of the proper court.

It is a fault if the bird falls short of the service court into the neutral area between the service court and net.

If the bird does not go over the net on the service it is a fault against the server.

Sue, the receiver, is called the "out" side. While receiving, she must stand with both feet within the boundaries of her service court until the server's racket strikes the bird.

The receiver faults if she hits the bird before it crosses the net to her side of the court.

It is a fault if a player hits the net with her racket or any part of her body during play.

If a player swings at a bird that is falling out of bounds but does not touch it, it is not a fault against that player. The bird is simply considered out of bounds.

But if he hits it, even though it would have fallen out of bounds, there is no fault and the bird is still in play.

It is a fault if a player hits the bird against obstructions above or around the court, such as ceilings, girders, walls, and so on.

If the bird is hit under the net during play, it is a fault.

If the bird hits a player during play, it is a fault against the player who is hit.

It is not a fault if the bird hits the top of the net and still lands within the proper playing area. The bird is considered in bounds both during play and on the service.

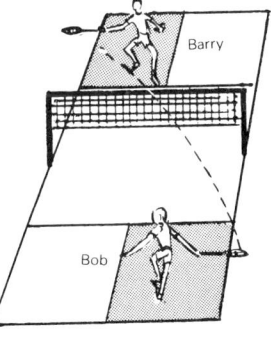

The first serve of every game is from the server's right hand service court into the receiver's right service court. Here Barry is the server. If he faults on his service, the service will go to Bob. But if Bob faults during the rally, Barry will serve again.

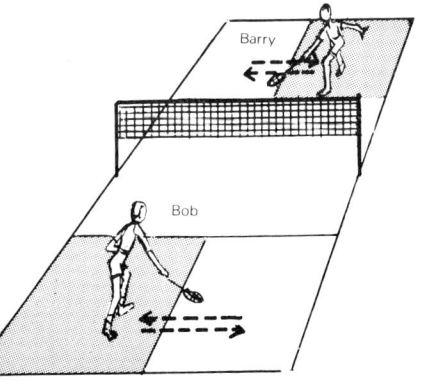

His next service will be from his left service court into Bob's left service court. If Barry wins this rally, his third serve will be from his right court again.

31

If, by mistake, he serves from the wrong court and his mistake is discovered before the next serve, it is called a "let" serve and he must try the serve again from the proper court. If it is not discovered until after the next serve, the mistake is ignored.

SCORING

YOU SCORE ONLY ON YOUR OWN SERVICE

Scoring in badminton is really very simple if you remember one important rule... you only score on your own service.

Here, for instance, Pam serves and Sue fails to return. Since Pam is the server, she scores one point. Now she will serve again and continue to serve alternating courts until she commits a fault. A turn at serving is called an "inning."

PAM SCORES A POINT

Here, however, Sue has returned Pam's serve and Pam can't return it to her. Sue does not get a point because she was not the server. Pam loses the serve. Sue becomes server. This is called a "hand out."

PAM LOSES SERVICE

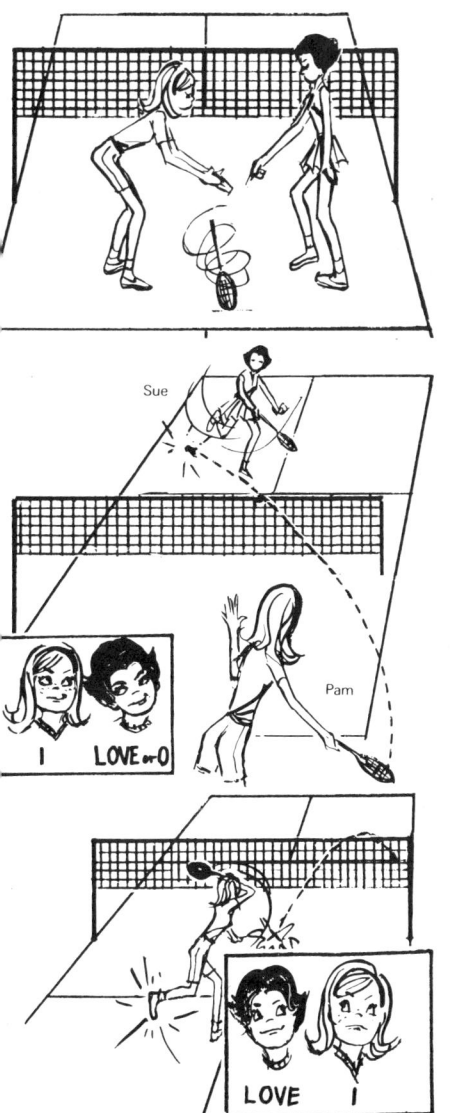

Let's see how this scoring works out in a game between Sue and Pam. To decide who serves first, they either toss a coin or spin a racket and call "rough" or "smooth." When Sue spins a racket Pam calls "rough" and the racket falls rough side up . . . that's the side where the trimming strings loop over the other ones. Now she can either serve first or let Sue serve first while she takes her choice of courts.

Pam decides to serve and on her first service Sue swings and misses. This is a point for Pam and the score is one-love. In badminton a score of nothing is called "love" and the server's score is always mentioned first.

On Pam's second serve she lifts one foot completely off the ground. This is a fault. A "hand out" is called and now Sue becomes server. The score is still love-one.

33

Sue starts her serve from her right court, but her first serve hits the post and is a fault. Now Pam gets the serve and the score is still one-love.

Pam starts her second turn at serving from the court she served from last in her last inning. This time the bird goes into the proper court but it touches the top of the net. This is a point for Pam.

Pam's next serve is good, but, as Sue returns it, it touches the top of the net and falls in bounds in Pam's court. Pam can't reach it so it's another hand out. The score is still love-two.

This time Sue serves deep into Pam's court and Pam misses. Because it's Sue's serve, she scores one point. The score is one to two, and Sue serves again.

34

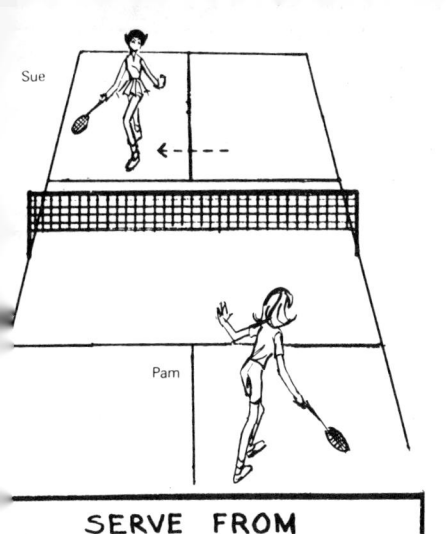

For her second serve she moves over to her left service court. Sue and Pam have a simple way of remembering the correct court for service during a game.

SERVE FROM	
LEFT COURT	RIGHT COURT
when score is	when score is
UNEVEN NUMBER	EVEN NUMBER
1-3-5 etc.	2-4-6 etc.

Here it is. You serve from your left court when your score is an uneven number. And serve from your right court when your score is an even number.

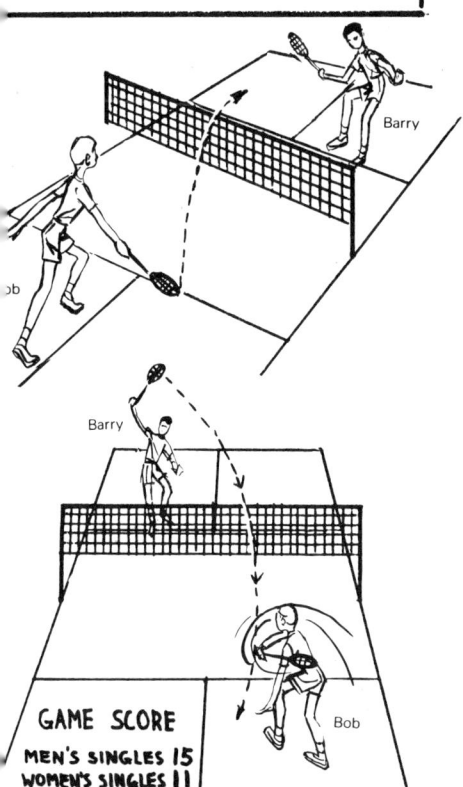

Barry and Bob continue play until one or the other player reaches game score of 15 points.

Game score for men's singles is fifteen points and for women's singles, eleven points. The first player to reach that score wins unless one player "sets" the game. Here is how a game can be set.

GAME SCORE
MEN'S SINGLES 15
WOMEN'S SINGLES 11

35

When a game is tied at thirteen all or fourteen all in men's singles or nine all or ten all in women's singles, the player who first reached the score may "set" the game to the number of points shown on this chart. After setting, the first player to win that number of points wins the game. For instance...

MEN' SINGLES
SCORE
13-13 may be set to 5 poin
14-14 may be set to 3 poin

WOMEN'S SINGLES
SCORE
9-9 may be set to 3 poin
10-10 may be set to 2 poin

...here it's Barry's serve and Bob fails to return. Barry scores a point and ties the score at thirteen all. Bob reached thirteen first so, instead of playing the game out to the normal fifteen points, he sets the game to five points.

That means the score now goes back to love all and the first player to win five points wins the game. If the score had been fourteen all, the first player to win three points would win the game.

DOUBLES PLAY

In doubles play, the procedure and scoring are similar to singles play, with a few additional rules. Let's watch part of this doubles game as Barry and Bob play against Cy and Don.

36

In the first inning Barry serves first. He is supposed to serve diagonally to the receiver's right court. But he serves into the receiver's left court, and that is a fault. In the **first** inning of doubles play, only one player of the team may serve, so now the service goes to Cy and Don.

Cy serves first in their inning and he faults. After the first inning in doubles, both players of the team have a turn of service in each inning so . . .

. . . even though Cy faulted, Don serves next. Since Cy failed in the right service court, Don serves from the left court.

He serves to Bob in the receiver's left service court, but Barry hits it first. This is a fault in doubles. So Don wins a point for his team and he can serve again.

He makes his next serve from the right service court. This time his bird hits the net. Now both Cy and Don have had a turn at serving during this inning, so the service goes back to Barry and Bob.

Barry serves first from the right service court because his team hasn't made its first point from that court. Just as in singles, Barry and Bob have an easy way of remembering which court they should be in for their service.

They remember their court position at the **beginning** of the game ... Bob on the left and Barry on the right as in the picture on the left. When their score is an even number they should be in this same position. When their score is an uneven number, their positions should be reversed, as in the picture on the right.

In doubles play it is a fault for more than one player to hit the bird before it goes back across the net. Here Cy and Don hit it in succession, so Barry and Bob score a point.

DOUBLES SETTING SCORES

score
13-13 may be set to 5 points
14-14 may be set to 3 points

In doubles, just as in singles, the game may be set at certain tied scores. At thirteen all, the first side to reach that score may set the game to five points. At fourteen all they may set it to three points. Then one side must score the required five or three points to win.

Barry, Bob, Cy and Don have a lot of real fun playing badminton. And their fun is greater because they know and obey the rules of the game.

This simple explanation of the more basic rules has not covered all of the fine points. If **you** want more fun from badminton and you wish to gain a fuller knowledge of the game, it would be a good idea to get a copy of the rule book and **keep** it handy.

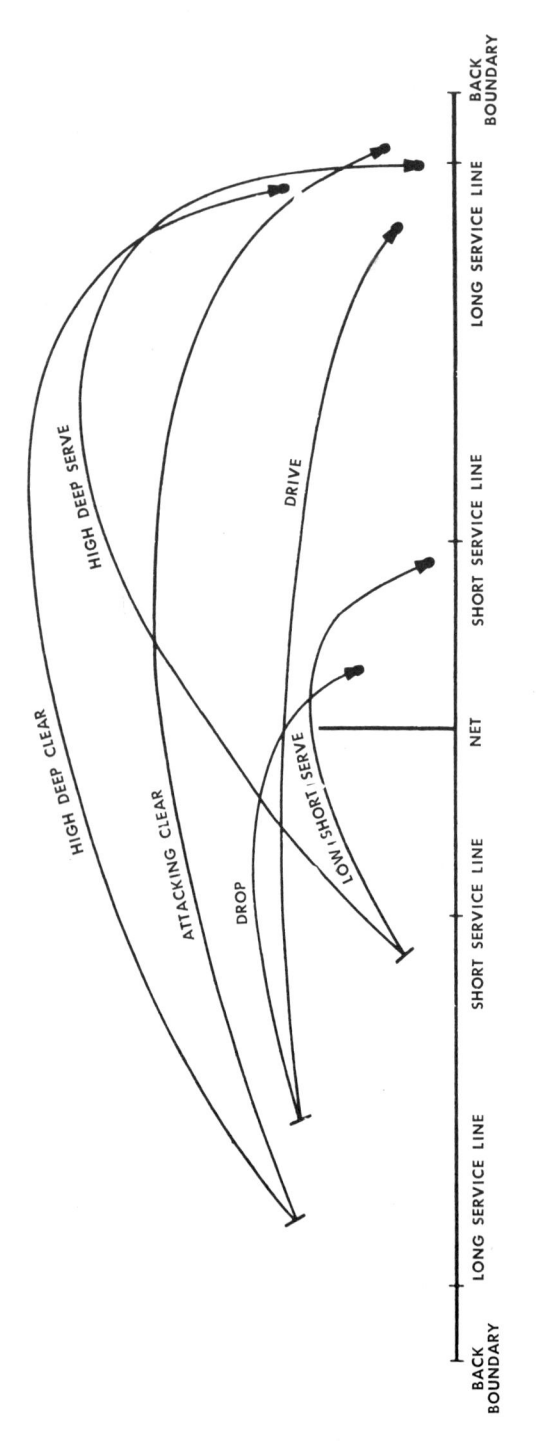

Diagram showing the path of some common badminton shots. The High Deep Clear is mostly a defensive weapon, used to force the opponent back from the net, and to gain time. The Attacking Clear serves the same purpose, but since it is lower and faster, it can be used on offense, since the opponent will have less time to move back under it.

The High Deep Serve is used mostly in singles play. It is aimed to drop the shuttle just inside of the back boundary line. The Low Short Serve is often used in doubles play, and is aimed to just clear the net and drop inside the short service line. The Drop is played so that the shuttle drops quickly downward as soon as it has passed over the net. The Drive is simply a hard-hit shuttle which moves almost parallel to the floor.

Not shown is the Smash, which is a shot on which the shuttle is hit sharply downward into the opponent's court. It can be seen that most of these shots can be made from any part of the court, and aimed to land almost anywhere in the opponent's court, depending upon the position of the opponent.

SOME COMMON BADMINTON TERMS

ACE: Any point scored, though usually said of a point scored on which a player failed to touch the shuttle with his racket.

ALLEY: The areas (one on each side of the court) which enlarge the court for doubles play. Each alley is 1½ feet wide, and runs the entire length of the court.

ALLEY SHOT: A shot which goes into the alley.

ATTACKING CLEAR: A type of clear (which see) which has a rather flat trajectory as it passes over the opponent's head.

BACK ALLEY: The area between the back boundary line and the long service line at the end of each half of the court. The shuttle may not be served into this area, which is 2½ feet deep, during doubles play.

BACK COURT: The general area near the back boundary lines.

BACKHAND: The stroke used to hit a shuttle which comes to the left side of a right-handed player, and to the right side of a left-handed player.

BACK-ROOM: Playing space to the rear of the court. There should be at least 5 or 6 feet of back-room between the back boundary line and any wall or other obstruction.

BALK: An attempt to throw an opponent off balance by feinting or by using false starts before or during a service attempt. If the server balks, he loses the service. If the receiver balks, he loses a point.

BAND: The canvas tape across the top of the badminton set. It is usually about 1½ inches wide.

BASE OF OPERATIONS: The spot on the court to which a player should move after making a shot so that he will be in the most advantageous position to reach his opponent's return. In singles play, this spot is in the center of the court, while in doubles play, it is the center of the area which the player is covering.

BIRD: A shuttle (which see).

CARRY: To hit the shuttle on the feathers rather than on the cork base. Such a hit will often cause the shuttle to tangle on the racket, or to be "slung" (which see). Hence it is a fault.

CHANGING COURTS: Players change courts at the start of the second game and at the start of the third game (if any) in a three-game match. During the third game, players change courts when one side first gains 8 points in a 15-point game, or 6 points in an 11-point game, or 11 points in a 21-point game.

CLEAR: A high, deep shot, aimed to go over the opponent's head, forcing him back from the net.

CROSS-COURT: Hitting the shuttle diagonally from one side of the court to the other, at an angle across the net.

DOUBLE HIT: Hitting the shuttle twice on the same stroke. It is a fault.

DOUBLES SERVICE LINE: A line, 2½ feet in from the back boundary line, beyond which the shuttle may not be served in doubles play. It is 19½ feet from the net. Once the shuttle has been served and returned, the Doubles Service Line has no significance during that particular rally.

DRIVE: A hard-hit shot, on which the shuttle travels low over the net with great speed, on a more or less horizontal line.

DRIVE SERVE: A hard-hit serve, with a flat trajectory.

END: A half of a badminton court. Hence, there are two ends, or "sides."

FACE: The hitting surface of the badminton racket.

FAST DROP: A shot which just clears the top of the net, and then drops quickly downward into the opponent's court.

FAULT: Any violation of the rules, or a playing error. A fault by the server results in loss of service. A fault by the receiver results in a point for the server.

FLIGHT: The path of the shuttle as it moves through the air.

FORE COURT: Generally, that area close to the net.

FOREHAND: The stroke used to hit a shuttle that comes to the right of a right-handed player, and to the left of a left-handed player.

FRAME: The part of the racket which holds the strings.

GAME: The usual game of badminton consists of 15 points for men and 11 points for women. A 21-point game can also be played. Ordinarily, the first player who gains the required number of points wins the game. However, when certain scoring conditions prevail, the point requirement can be changed by "Setting" (which see). These scoring methods are explained in the section covering the rules. During any game, a point may be made only by the serving side.

HAIRPIN: A shot which starts close to the floor near the net, rises up over the net and drops sharply downward. So called because of its shape.

HALF COURT SHOT: A low shot which drops into the middle of the opponent's court.

HAND-IN: The person or side which has the service is "hand-in." Often shortened to "In."

HAND-OUT: The person or side which receives the serve is "hand-out." Often shortened to "Out."

HEAD-ROOM: The space above the court which is free from obstructions. In order to prevent the shuttle from striking any overhead object as it is hit during normal play, there should be at least 25 feet of unobstructed space above the court.

HIGH DEEP CLEAR: A type of clear (which see) which rises very high into the air and drops to the rear of the opponent's court. It is usually made as a defensive measure.

HIGH DEEP SERVE: A high, arching serve which drops just within the back boundary line.

IN: A shot which lands, or would have landed, within the proper playing area, is said to be "In." Also short for "Hand-In" (which see).

INNING: The time during which a player or side holds the service. Similar to "Hand-In" (which see).

LIFT: A stroke made close to the net, in order to boost the shuttle safely up and over the net.

LINES: The markings (1½ inches wide) which define the boundaries and sections of the court. A shuttle which lands on a line is considered to have landed in the area which the line defines.

LOVE: Zero. A score of "Six-Love" means that the server has six points and his opponent has no points. The server's score is always mentioned first.

LOW SHORT SERVE: A type of serve which just clears the net and lands in the front portion of the service court.

MATCH: A badminton match is ordinarily the best two-out-of-three games.

MATCH POINT: That point which, if won by the server, wins the match for him.

MISS: Failure to hit the shuttle with the racket. It is not a fault if the server misses the shuttle completely while attempting to serve. During play, a contestant can swing at the shuttle and miss it as many times as he wants to before he hits it, without a fault, but there is seldom any reason to do so.

MIX UP: To continually vary the type and force of strokes used during the game, in order to keep the opponent guessing.

NET: The badminton net is 2½ feet deep, and stretches across the center of the entire court. At the center of the court, the top of the net should be 5 feet from the floor. It should be 5 feet 1 inch at the posts on the side boundary lines.

ONE OUT: A term used to remind the players in a doubles game that one member of the serving team has had his turn at service, and that the serve will change sides as soon as the remaining server is retired.

OUT: A shuttle which lands outside of the boundary lines of the proper court section is said to be "Out." Also short for "Hand-Out" (which see).

PASSING SHOT: A shot which goes past an opponent to the side, as contrasted to a shot which goes over his head.

PLACEMENT: A shot which the opponent cannot touch with his racket before it strikes the court surface.

POINT: A unit of scoring. Only the server or serving side can score a point. Points are scored when the receiver faults or fails to touch the serve.

POONA: The original name for badminton. The game of badminton originated in India, was introduced into England in the 1870's and into America around 1900.

RACKET: There are no official rules governing the measurements of a badminton racket. However, the ordinary racket is about 26 inches long, and has a hitting surface, or face, which is about 9½ inches long and 8 inches wide. A racket usually weighs from 3.7 to 5 ounces.

RALLY: The continual play between the time a shuttle is served and one player faults.

RECEIVER: The receiver of a serve must stand within the service court diagonally opposite the server. He must stay within this service court until the server hits the shuttle. In doubles play, the partner of the receiver can stand at any point.

RETRIEVE: Primarily defensive play.

RIGHT SERVICE COURT: The service court to a player's right as he faces the net. In singles play, the players serve from and receive in their respective Right Service Courts when the server's score is zero or an even number of points. When the server's score is an odd number of points, the server serves and the receiver receives in their respective Left Service Courts. In a doubles game, the first service of a side in each inning is made from the right service court, and alternates until the side is retired, except that the side beginning a game has only one hand in its first inning.

ROUGH: The term "Rough" is applied to that side of a badminton racket on which the small binding strips at the top and bottom of the face of the racket form loops around the regular strings. The other side is known as "Smooth." Spinning a racket and guessing "rough" or "smooth" is one way of determining which side will serve first to which court, etc.

RUSHING: Moving in quickly to the net to smash the shuttle down into the opponent's court.

SERVE: To put the shuttle into play. A player is allowed only one serve for each point.

SETTING: Changing the number of points required to win a game. A game may be set when the score becomes tied with one or two points to go. When that happens, the person who first reached the particular score has the right to prolong the game by adding points, if he so desires. The procedure and requirements for "Setting" a game are outlined in the section on rules.

SHAFT: The part of the racket between the head and the handle.

SHORT: A shot which fails to reach its mark, such as a serve which falls in front of the proper service court.

SHUTTLE: The "ball" of badminton. Essentially, a shuttle consists of a rounded piece of cork into which about 15 feathers are symmetrically arranged. Because of their peculiar constructions, shuttles vary appreciably in size, weight and flight characteristics. Shuttles are also known as "birds", or by the correct name of "shuttlecock."

SLING: To allow the racket to contact the shuttle for too long a time, so that the shuttle is carried on the racket and "slung" rather than hit sharply and cleanly. It is a fault.

SMASH: A hard, overhead shot which drives the shuttle sharply downward.

THROAT: That part of the racket where the handle joins the head.

THROW: Same as "Sling."

TOSS SERVE: The usual type of badminton serve, in which the shuttle is tossed or dropped out in front of the server, who hits it as it descends.

TOUCHING THE NET: Contacting the net with the racket or the body. It is a fault.

VOLLEY: To hit the shuttle while it is in the air and before it touches the ground. Hence, all legal badminton shots must be volleyed.

WIDE: Said of a shot which lands out of the court along the side boundaries.

PLAYING BETTER BADMINTON

Singles

The ability to serve or return a shuttle with a properly-executed stroke is the basic requirement for playing a good game of badminton. However, this ability must be combined with a knowledge of game strategy, for the nicely-executed stroke accomplishes little if your opponent has no trouble in returning your shot.

Hence, on every badminton stroke, you should think not only of **how** to hit the shuttle, but **where** to hit it. Here are a few basic principles of playing strategy which you should remember during singles play:

(1) **Mix up your shots. You can keep your opponent off balance if you vary your returns — drives, clears, drops, and smashes.**

(2) A player who has to run to make a recovery will usually not be able to make a perfect return, so aim your shots as far away from your opponent as possible. This means that you have to practice hitting the shuttle so that you can consistently place it within a foot or two of the spot you aim at. Often, however, it is smart to hit the shuttle directly at your opponent, particularly if he is close to the net, since such a return is very difficult to handle properly.

(3) **After you make your shot, try to move to a position which will enable you to cover the area to which your opponent's return will probably come. Generally, this position will be at the center of your court.**

(4) When serving, put your opponent on the defensive by serving long, forcing him back from the net. Serve short occasionally to keep him guessing.

(5) **When your opponent puts you in hot water by rushing the net or by forcing you to do considerable running to make a return, clear the shuttle by lobbing it over the opponent's head. This will force him back, and give you time to get set for his return. When clearing, try to hit the shuttle just over your opponent's head, allowing him less time to get back under your shot.**

(6) Do not try to smash unless you are reasonably close to the net.

(7) **Be alert at all times, and keep your eye on the shuttle as you hit it.**

Doubles

Doubles play presents some additional problems, for teammates must decide on the court areas which each should cover. Such players have their choice of playing side by side, or moving one player up to cover the front part of the court while the other player protects the back part of the court, or playing a combination of these two systems.

There are advantages and disadvantages to each formation, and players should experiment with each to find these good and bad features. As a general rule, a doubles team should be side by side on defense, and up and back on offense.

In other words, if you have the other team in trouble, it is smart to move a player up close to the net so that he can make a rally-winning smash on poor returns by the other team. If your team is in trouble, playing side by side will enable you to protect the doubles alley and still be in position to move up to the net to return a drop or a rapidly-descending smash.

Whatever system is used, partners should have some sort of rule or signal to keep both players from trying to return the same shot. In general, the same offensive tactics for singles play apply to doubles play — keep your opponents off balance, keep your opponents guessing.

---

notes

notes

notes

notes

GV
1007
.B23

GV
1007
.B23